Salisbury
in old picture postcards

by
Alan A. Richardson

European Library - Zaltbommel/Netherlands MCMLXXXIII

To Pauline – my wife, for coming to love Salisbury as much as I do.

About the author:
The author was born in Salisbury and returned there after spending 28 years in London with the B.B.C. Television Service. Now he is a registered guide with the West Country Tourist Board, a member of the Guild of Guide Lecturers, a free-lance writer for Radio and sundry magazines, and is a Member of the British Academy of Film and Television Arts.
Join him on a nostalgic tour round his lovely home town, and with the help of these old postcards compare what you see today with how it was nearly one hundred years ago.

GB   ISBN 90 288 2460 x

European Library in Zaltbommel/Netherlands publishes among other things the following series:

IN OLD PICTURE POSTCARDS *is a series of books which sets out to show what a particular place looked like and what life was like in Victorian and Edwardian times. A book about virtually every town in the United Kingdom is to be published in this series. By the end of this year about 75 different volumes will have appeared. 1,250 books have already been published devoted to the Netherlands with the title* **In oude ansichten.** *In Germany, Austria and Switzerland 500, 60 and 15 books have been published as* **In alten Ansichten;** *in France by the name* **En cartes postales anciennes** *and in Belgium as* **En cartes postales anciennes** *and/or* **In oude prentkaarten** *150 respectively 400 volumes have been published.*

For further particulars about published or forthcoming books, apply to your bookseller or direct to the publisher.

This edition has been printed and bound by Grafisch Bedrijf De Steigerpoort in Zaltbommel/Netherlands.

INTRODUCTION

Welcome to all of you who have decided to visit our lovely city of Salisbury. Stay a few hours, preferably days, and let me help you to explore and get to know something of the history of our ancient town and surrounding countryside. There is lots to see. Some of you will have travelled across the world to visit us, others may live only a few miles away and feel it is high time to find out a little more about the city that you probably visit often on business or for shopping, but rarely seem to have the time to explore in depth. Well – take two hours off and join me, and with the aid of this little book of old postcards, come on a walk-about round our streets and lanes. After all the Queen has done it, a prime-minister has done it, they both enjoyed it too, for you it will probably be a little less crowded!

Take a moment and sit awhile in the Market Square and absorb the atmosphere of this ancient city that has seen so much history take place within its boundaries down through the years. Today the city is host to some 37,000 inhabitants, they mostly make a living from agriculture, and supplying the needs of the city and its hinterland of some 130,000 country folk. The Church and the military (strange bed-fellows you might think) also employ many citizens, for Salisbury and its great cathedral is an important centre of religious life, and the military training areas all around have been with us since the days of the Crimea. There is a little light industry in the locality, and the railway still plays an important part in the communications network of the south and west. Trade is its lifeblood however, and ever since Henry III gave us a Charter in 1227, and the bridges were built across the many rivers surrounding Salisbury, trade has flowed in and out of the city, bringing wealth to many, and a reasonable living to most. Our closeness to the channel ports of Southampton and Portsmouth has meant a cultural and commercial link with France and the rest of Europe has been maintained for hundreds of years. During the middle-ages our wool from the thousands of sheep reared on the grass uplands of Salisbury Plain was much sought after. Charles II always insisted on having Salisbury cloth for his waistcoats, and we certainly know today the power of royal patronage in the world of fashion, so it must have been quite a boost for our local cloth industry when Charles II was so taken with our home product.

In modern times Salisbury plays host to many hundreds of young visitors from all over Europe who come to learn our language in the local schools during the summer holidays. Very welcome they are too, their colourful chatter in so many different tongues and their youthful exuberance lend a cosmopolitan flavour to the otherwise somewhat dignified way of life of this old cathedral city.

It is not only overseas students and visitors that have taken to the habit of visiting our fair city. Down the centuries kings and queens of England have found Salisbury a useful stopping place as they travelled their kingdom. In some ways the people of Salisbury became the ping pong balls in the game of royal politics, bounced back and forth across the green grass table of southern England, as the power game was played out, monarchs sometimes winning, sometimes losing – their heads! Anything for a quiet life the citizens wisely offered their allegiance to whichever monarch was in power at the particular time they were passing through the city. Needless to say during the Civil War it all became rather confusing for the city fathers, as Royalists and Roundheads skirmished within the city boundaries, but eventually these turbulent times passed, and in later years royalty tended to come for social rather than political reasons. The great country seats of Wilton House, Longford Castle, and Trafalgar House offered attractive hunting, shooting and fishing for their royal guests.

For Salisbury folk all these visits seem to crystallize into a sparkling welcome when in 1974 our present Queen came for the Royal Maundy Ceremony in the cathedral. This gentle and picturesque religious pageant was a joy to behold and listen to, and afterwards the Queen moved on to the Guidhall in the Market Square, near perhaps to where you are sitting now, for a luncheon of hare pâté and roast Wiltshire pork, a 'morsel for a monarch' indeed! Like all those who appreciate a stroll after a good meal she went afterwards on a walkabout through our city streets. Hundreds of well-wishers came forward to 'shake hands with a Queen upon the Throne', and she to say a word or two to each of them in turn, perhaps 'a carefree word with a little nonsense in it now and then does not misbecome a Monarch'. If some of the ladies in the crowds were more interested in her hat than in the reasons for her presence in the city that day, then this was only natural for it was H.G. Wells who wrote 'the British Crown is not like any other Crown, it may conceivably take a line of it's own and emerge possibly a little more like a hat and a little less like a crown from trials that may destroy every other monarchial system in the world'. This indeed is the monarchy of our times, truly the monarch of the market place! But then you never know who may be seen wandering round the market place in Salisbury. A few years ago you might well have brushed shoulders with that great Hollywood star of the 1930's, the ever discreet Greta Garbo, as she searched out antiques in the little shops around the square accompanied by her great friend the late Sir Cecil Beaton who used to live nearby.

Now that you have sat awhile in the busy heart of Salisbury, described so vividly by Charles Dickens in his book 'Martin Chuzzlewit' and by W.H. Hudson in his book 'A Shepherds Life', you will have absorbed some of the flavour of this busy market town and the vitality of its life. Lets up and away and explore the streets and lanes of the city, and with the aid of this motley collection of old postcards and photographs, mostly fifty or more years old, we can compare what we see today with what people saw yesteryear.

Grateful acknowledgements are made to all those early publishers of postcards nearly a century ago. Most have now disappeared, but great names such as Raphael Tuck of London, J. Salmon of Sevenoaks, and F. Frith of Reigate are still with us. Locally names such as Jukes, Jefferies, Mullins, Newman, and Edwards have all now gone, but it is pleasing to record that the old family business of F. Futcher and Son is still thriving in Fisherton Street. Thanks are also due to the Salisbury College of Art, the Salisbury Museum, and Methuen and Co for their help. I am sure all of the original publishers of the cards in this little book would be delighted to know that those old pictures are still looked at with increasing interest and affection for the old days they so graphically portray. As you wander round our city you will find that some streets have changed little for Salisbury prides itself on guarding the historic character of its ancient heart, other streets will be barely recognisable so different they have become, but whether the city is viewed through your eyes today, or through the eyes of those who have lived and loved our city long ago, Salisbury's welcome is as warm as ever, and is glad to share her unique charms with you today. Let us then take a closer look at this Market Square as we turn the pages on.

THE CATTLE MARKET, SALISBURY.

1. Salisbury is dominated by the cathedral and the Market Square. Let us take a look at some different viewpoints of this busy central meeting place. The parish church of St. Thomas' is seen beyond the trees. The statue is Lord Herbert of Lea, but you won't see him there now for when the 1914-1918 war memorial was built Lord Herbert was given a home in Victoria Park.

Market Place, Salisbury

2. Cattle and sheep dominated the Tuesday markets until the 1950's when a new cattle market was built to the north of the city. The statue half hidden midway along the avenue of stalls on the left is that of Sir Henry Fawcett. In 1858 he was blinded in a shooting accident, despite this he became a Member of Parliament and eventually the Postmaster General, and was the creator of Britain's Parcel Post Service. He died in 1884.

SALISBURY, THE MARKET PLACE   75601

3. This is a 1920's view of the Tuesday market with some interesting motor vehicles parked around the statue as well as the ice-cream van on the right. We still have one that attends the market regularly. The clothing stalls are as popular as the pens of sheep beyond the trees.

4. A similar view but a Saturday market day this time and some splendid buses and char-a-bancs of the late 1920's parked ready to take the shoppers back to their villages scattered along the river valleys radiating from the city.

SALISBURY. — *The Council Chambers*.

5. The Guildhall, sometimes called the Council Chambers, in 1900. Six Tuscan columns support the portico and the arched windows are surrounded by deeply indented stones known as heavy rustication. The right hand window gives light to a splendid banqueting room, the rest contains the law courts so you enter the building with mixed feelings depending upon your business for that particular day!

6. Within the shadows of the Guildhall our Queen went on a walk-about around the Market Square in 1974 when she visited the city for the Royal Maundy Service in the cathedral. She met many of the citizens and today personifies 'the Monarch in the Market Place'. This picture is kindly supplied by Salisbury's long established newspaper The Journal, first published in 1729. Get a copy today and find out what is going on in the city.

7. The Square was used for many purposes other than the market. Occasionally as many as 4 000 men would sit down to an open air dinner to celebrate a jubilee, a coronation, or a peace thanksgiving. The giant Hob Nob, its origin somewhat steeped in mystery, would survey the scene, perhaps wondering why no ladies were present! Equality of the sexes had not yet arrived in Salisbury!

8. Down the centuries, by virtue of another Charter granted by Henry III in 1270 a three day fair now celebrates the Feast of Saint Remigius. Today everyone flocks to the Square to ride the round-about, the big wheel, and ever more exciting space age machines.

SALISBURY. THE MARKET PLACE

V6176

9. On the north side of the Market Square is Blue Boar Row, a wide thoroughfare lined with banks, shops and restaurants. Here the buses for the city centre routes start today as they did in the thirties. The Victorian-Greek façade in the distance once belonged to the Market House Railway, then the shortest privately owned railway in Britain. Now it has become our superb Public Library and Art Gallery.

CITY OF SALISBURY.

COPYRIGHT.

Salisbury Cathedral from the Avon

10. The Arms of the City of New Sarum has the Latin inscription 'Civitas Novae Sarum' to distinguish it from the former city of Salisbury that was built atop the hill a mile to the north on the road to Stonehenge, and the Arms consist of four bars of blue and gold, with double-headed eagles, ducally crowned as supporters. Let us take a look at that original city in the next three pictures.

OLD SARUM CASTLE

11. From this early aerial view the two great circular ditches are clearly defined with the foundations of the original cathedral top left. The inner Norman fortress had a bridge across the inner ditch. Even before the Romans came to Britain in A.D. 41 this hill-top was a defended position guarding the many tracks that criss-crossed the great chalk uplands of Salisbury Plain.

General View of Excavations at Old Sarum.

12. In the early 1900's major excavations took place on the hill-top to uncover the remains of the Norman fortress. Walls, dungeons, kitchens and wells were unearthed enabling a picture of life as it was in that great castle to be vividly re-created. Magnificient views of the new city and surrounding countryside are seen from the battlements, for the narrow track makes a spectacular walk that all should take.

13. This picture is of a model of Old Sarum that is on exhibition in Salisbury Museum in the Cathedral Close. It shows the cathedral and the Norman castle as well as the hundreds of little houses crowded within the safety of the outer ditch. Modern thinking suggests that probably there were fewer houses within the walls and far more outside stretching down the hill.

SALISBURY CATHEDRAL FROM THE MEADOWS

14. Old Sarum eventually fell into ruins because at the bottom of the hill among the lush water-meadows the new cathedral of Bishop Poore was built between 1220 and 1258, and later in 1330 its 404 foot high spire soared as a symbol of Christ towards the heavens. Its magnificence and beautiful setting made it a subject of countless artists down the centuries.

SALISBURY CATHEDRAL

15. The sailing barge reminds us of the times when the River Avon was navigable down to the sea, and goods would be transported, cheaply if slowly, by water. The Purbeck marble for the Cathedral probably was shipped to Salisbury by barge from Christchurch where the Avon meets the sea. Promises of a proper canal to the sea never materialised however.

SALISBURY CATHEDRAL.

16. Elm trees — most of them have now disappeared — are seen here dotted around the wide lawns of the superb Close. Today a few have survived as well as the cedars of Lebanon which are hundreds of years old. The west front is richly adorned with stone carvings of Our Lord, the apostles, angels and saints, and cathedral worthies from past centuries.

Salisbury Cathedral

17. This view from the north-east shows the full beauty and the purity of the early English gothic style, achieved by completing the building within the short space of 38 years, from 1220 to 1258. This means the cathedral must have been well endowed with funds in order to employ such a large work-force, and thereby completing the vast undertaking so quickly.

Salisbury Cathedral, The Cloisters

F. G. O. Stuart. 714

18. Salisbury cathedral has the largest and most beautiful cloisters in England. Two Lebanese cedars cast their shade upon the green lawns within, known as the Garth. The Chapter House seen beyond the cloisters is today the Treasury and contains not only superb silver from all over the diocese but Salisbury's own copy of Magna Carta signed by King John in 1215.

19. The Bishop's Palace where for several centuries the bishops had lived, except for a short period after the Civil War of 1646 when Oliver Cromwell billeted Roundhead troops there, turning it into an inn. Today small boys sing, work, and play within its beautiful rooms, the ancient crypt and great hall echoing to the music of the cathedral choir school.

S 1831

CLOSE GATE, SALISBURY.

20. The Cathedral Close is surrounded by a wall on three sides, and the River Avon on the fourth. Three gates give access to the walled community in which several hundred people live. Every night at 11 p.m. the gates are shut and locked! The busiest gate is that on the north side opening on to the High Street. Within the niche above the arch a statue of King Edward VII surveys the scene.

IN THE CLOSE, SALISBURY.

21. Just inside the High Street gate is the College of Matrons. Built by Bishop Seth Ward in 1682 the design is attributed to Sir Christopher Wren. The story goes that the bishop channelled his ardour into building this lovely Alms House when a certain lady refused his love and offer of marriage. To this day widows of the clergy have sanctuary within its walls. What a nice man he must have been!

22. Chorister's Green on the north side of the Close is overlooked by Mompesson House, a lovely William and Mary house built in 1701, now owned by the National Trust and open to the public. For a short time in the late 1940's it became the Bishop's Palace. Children from nearby schools still play upon the grass sixty years on from when this picture was taken.

Salisbury, "The Wardrobe" in the Close

23. Beyond Chorister's Green on the western side we pass a superb mediaeval building named the Bishop's Wardrobe. In times past the bishop would store within the goods he received by way of taxation from the townspeople, the proceeds of which went towards the upkeep of the church. Today it is a fascinating military museum depicting the history of the local county regiments. Well worth a visit!

SALISBURY SPIRE
FROM CANONRY GARDEN

24. Just beyond the Military Museum you pass the
North Canonry. It seems an ever open door beckons
you into a lovely secret garden with an herbaceous
border-lined walk down to the river. Savour its
beauty and peace and put something in the box on
the way out to help those who work so hard to make
it so lovely, and who wish to share its beauty with
you.

THE KINGS HOUSE TRAINING COLLEGE, SALISBURY.

25. Still moving down the west side of the Close you come to the King's House, that once was the College of Sarum St. Michael mentioned in Thomas Hardy's 'Jude the Obscure'. Today the King's House, so named because various monarchs had tarried there and held assemblies, is the new home of the museum, an essential place to visit and enjoy its superb galleries of exhibits of local treasures from the past.

Salisbury
Lover's Walk

26. Finally on the western side you end up in a little cul-de-sac immediately before the present home of the bishop, a picturesque corner of the Close, and at one time judging by this early postcard, a favourite walk for the young in heart.

27. Back on the north side of the Close walking east you pass today the same red pillar box as you walk towards St. Anne's Gate. The maid in cap and apron suggests more leisurely times. Is she reading the racing results? Or maybe a message from a boy friend?

IN THE CLOSE, SALISBURY.

28. Again a few yards down from that same letter box you pass the tall square house on the corner, now a school for little children. Once it was the home of a local writer who wrote an enchanting memoir of her childhood living within the cloistered life of the Close entitled 'The Children of the Close'. You can still find this delightful book in second hand bookshops – if you are lucky!

Theological Hall, Salisbury

29. Near to St. Anne's Gate is the Theological College founded in 1860, where young men train for the priesthood. Today it is combined with that of the cathedral of Wells, alongside is their flint and stone chapel.

30. St. Anne's Gate leads from the city into the Close on the eastern side of the town. In the room above the arch, Handel the composer is said to have worked whilst staying with the Harris family who lived alongside in Malmesbury House. In the little house on the left of the arch Henry Fielding lived and wrote his famous book 'Tom Jones' whilst married to a Salisbury girl.

Harnham or
South Gate

SALISBURY.

31. Harnham Gate opens on to the south side of the city and within a few minutes you
are in the countryside atop of Harnham Hill. There were, and still are, many small schools
within the Close, and no doubt the children playing in the picture are from one of them.

32. From the parapet of the cathedral tower a splendid view is obtained of the city below. The modern development of car stacks and shopping precincts are all built in warm red brick to merge into the general mediaeval character of the city. Notice too the lovely secret gardens hidden away between the walls of the old houses. During the summer the cathedral tower is open to visitors three times per day.

The Close Gate
Salisbury

Barness

33. Let us now leave the Cathedral Close and explore the busy city streets. Coming out of the High Street, or North Gate, we enter a busy shopping street, although this picture would suggest a quieter period in our history! Today huge motor coaches full of visitors squeeze through the narrow entrance. The gates were built in 1330 with the stones from the old cathedral on the hill top at Old Sarum.

S 1823   HIGH STREET, SALISBURY.

34. From bicycle to early motor cars! This view of the High Street from the bottom looking towards the cathedral gate shows a vehicle heralding in the new motor age, looking quite futuristic among the horse-drawn carts. Notice too the gas lamps outside the shop on the left. The corner building used to be the Assembly Rooms, venue for concerts and grand balls, now a modern bookshop.

SALISBURY, HIGH STREET   59015

35. The same street further up towards the cathedral gate. The motor car is maturing!
Street lighting is still with gas. The George Hotel remains today but as a restaurant, the
Crown Hotel on the right has gone. A barrel organ entertains but there is no sign of a
monkey! At the top on the left take note of the corner-house with a bishop's mitre on
the wall. Next page tells you why.

36. Today the corner shop is still known as Mitre House where Bishop Poore, who built the cathedral in 1220, lived. Since 1451 to this day a charming custom prevails whenever there is a new bishop of Salisbury. On his enthronement day he will enrobe in this shop as a token of esteem for that first bishop and then walk in procession to his cathedral. Bishop Baker, flanked by Dean and Precentor, are doing just this in 1982.

37. The Old George Hotel in the High Street, a hostelry since the fourteenth century. Elizabeth I did not sleep there but infamous Oliver Cromwell, and famous diarist Samuel Pepys did! Now part of a restaurant complex the beautiful panelled rooms are still in use on the first floor, but the ground floor rooms have become the entrance to the modern shopping precinct.

The old George Hotel, Salisbury. An early 14th Century Inn.

Old George Hotel, Salisbury.

38. Inside the Old George Hotel we see one of the first floor sitting rooms, with its wood-panelled chimney breast, plastered beams, and if only walls could speak what stories they could tell of past visitors who have enjoyed its comforts down through the years. Unlicensed in the thirties it became a favourite with visiting clergy, but wine flowed freely from across the street, born aloft by waiters dodging the traffic between dining room and pub!

THE GARDEN at the OLD GEORGE HOTEL, SALISBURY.
Formerly a part of the courtyard in which the Strolling Players used to perform their plays.

39. This garden today is a part of the Old George Shopping Mall. William Shakespeare wrote 'As You Like It' in 1599 for Lord Pembroke at Wilton House two miles away. Could it be that the final rehearsal for that premiere production took place in this very spot for a local by-law insisted that the strolling players stayed at the Old George when visiting Salisbury?

SILVER STREET, SALISBURY

40. At the bottom of the High Street turn right into Silver Street. Here the silversmiths had their workshops and made the scissors and cutlery that Salisbury became famous for in the eighteenth century and before. To this day in Sheffield, the home of British cutlery making, they refer to 'Salisbury longs' and 'Salisbury shorts' when describing the size of different knives.

POULTRY CROSS AND SILVER STREET, SALISBURY

A SERIES OF 25

Nº 11

THE
GROWING OF TOBACCO
IN ENGLAND
ENABLES US TO OFFER
AT POPULAR PRICES
THE NOW CELEBRATED

BLUE PRYOR BRAND
OF TOBACCO & CIGARETTES

This new industry gives employment in Agricultural England to 3000 men & women
to every 1000 acres planted.

"ENGLAND FOR THE ENGLISH"
Therefore let England produce the Tobacco smoked
by Englishmen, thereby giving employment to the men
& women of our Motherland.

H. STEVENS & Cº
TOBACCO FACTORY,
SALISBURY

41. Looking along Silver Street from the other direction we see a late twenties local Wilts and Dorset bus coming towards the Poultry Cross. Stevens tobacco factory was just beyond the Cross on the right above what is now a modern dress shop. Cigarettes and pipe tobacco were manufactured there from 1780 until the 1960's. Stevens issued their own cigarette cards so popular among young boys in the 1920's and 1930's.

HIGH STREET & POULTRY CROSS, SALISBURY.

20564

42. The Poultry Cross, the only surviving one of four such market crosses in Salisbury. Built in the early fourteenth century, the actual origins are somewhat obscure, but it seems certain that the crosses had a religious significance in addition to commercial usage in their early days. Here the A.A. patrolman directs the traffic on a busy market day in the early 1930's.

Fish Market.   Salisbury.

43. Beyond the Poultry Cross eastwards stretches
Butchers Row, Fish Row and Ox Row, where those
trades were carried on. Few of the picturesque houses
seen in this picture by Marjorie C. Bates survive to this
day. Amazingly the previous picture shows two-way
traffic in this narrow street, today it is a pedestrian-
way only.

Minster St., Salisbury, looking N.

44. Looking north from the Poultry Cross is Minster Street, with a fine row of timbered gabled houses with oriel bay windows, including the celebrated Chop House, the Haunch of Venison built in 1320, and still a favourite meeting place for farmers visiting the city on market days. The public bar only seats two people but there is plenty of room elsewhere in this ancient tavern.

45. Minster Street looking the other way southwards. This print from an old book on Salisbury shows the stream down one side and the
efforts being made to keep the water flowing to
clear the refuse, not with much success for
these streams became open drains and a health
hazard until bricked over in the 1850's. The
houses on the right are little changed to this
day.

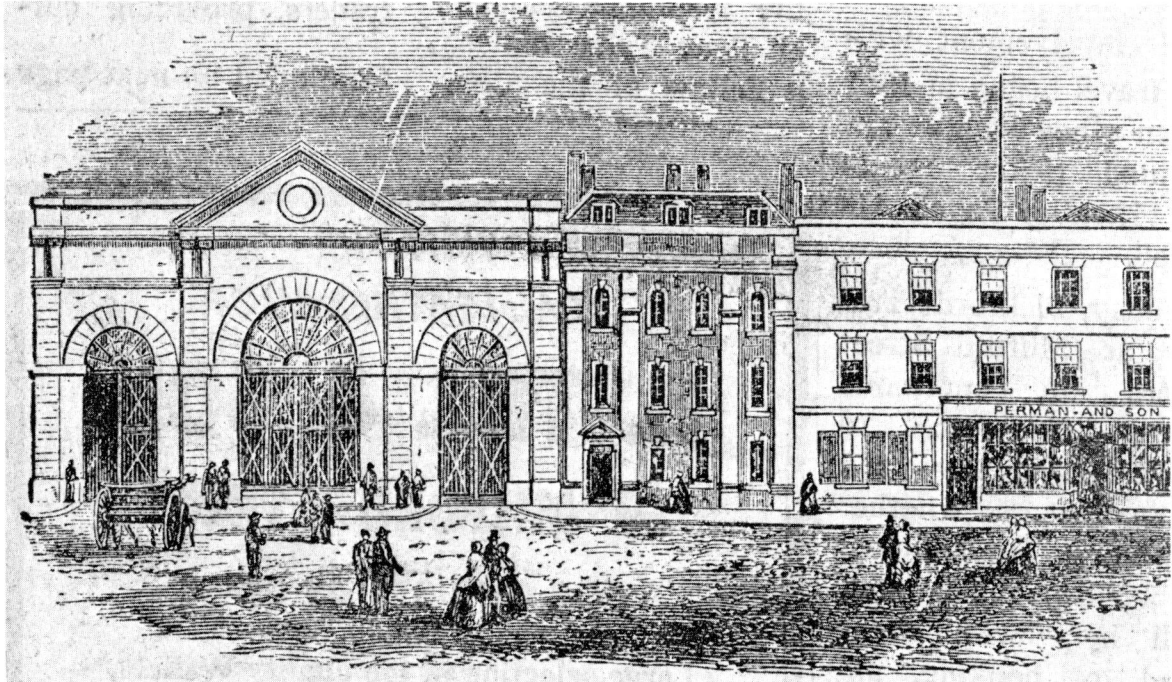

46. At the end of Minster Street walking north we pass the old cheese market on the left and the still apparent neo-classic frontage of what is now our splendid Public Library, but what was originally the Market House and Railway. Built in 1859 to bring in the produce from the local countryside to auction in the Market House, it was for a while the shortest privately owned railway in Britain running for a quarter of a mile to the main line. It became derelict in the 1920's when marketing techniques changed and then eventually it became the city's library.

47. North from the Public Library runs Castle Street. This picture from an old book, published about 1800, shows the sheep and cattle being driven to the central Market Square, with another of those streams (no wonder Salisbury was called the Venice of southern England!) running down the right hand side with a lady busy washing! A giant supermarket and the post office dominate the scene today!

CASTLE STREET, SALISBURY.

48. This picture is in marked contrast to the previous one showing Castle Street in the 1920's with the entrance to the New Theatre clearly visible. Here touring companies put on weekly plays, and then the early movies arrived, until in 1932 it closed when the big new super cinemas were built. Cattle were still driven past to market and it wasn't unknown for a bull to stray into the cinema and for a brave manageress to eject it!

60 SALISBURY. — *Queen Street.*

49. Returning to the market place on the eastern side lies Queen Street and this picture shows a busy scene on a market day in about 1900. The façades of most of the houses on the left have survived to this day. The sign 'Turkish Baths' marks the entrance to the Cross Keys Chequer of today, a modern shopping precinct.

50. Beyond Queen Street northwards lies Endless Street. Here was the Palace Theatre built in 1889, and finally closing in 1931, giving way to a garage and then an office block on the corner. The splendid old bus for Larkhill started from this point. Today the modern bus station is opposite. Grateful thanks to Mrs. Sanger for the use of this old photograph.

CATHERINE STREET, SALISBURY.

51. Going southwards again back down Queen Street and straight across the junction you come to Catherine Street, originally named Carter's Street. Through the years it has always been a busy area of small shops and little restaurants. The house where I was born is still in this street, and my young eyes must have looked out upon a very similar scene to this postcard of the early twenties.

ST. ANNE'S GATE, ST. JOHN'S STREET, SALISBURY   8575

52. Further south of Catherine Street you come into St. John's Street, looking north-wards from St. Anne's Gate. Malmesbury House is on the left, its windows piercing the original Close wall built in 1330. Opposite is the Kings Arms Hotel where loyalists to Charles II planned his escape to France, during Cromwell's time. Legend has it that Charles hid in the room with the oriel bay window on the left and escaped by a secret passage to the inn, but he was in fact hiding in Heale House five miles away.

Joiners Hall, St. Anns Street, Salisbury.

53. Leading off, opposite St. Anne's Gate, is St. Anne's Street. Originally this was the road to Southampton. On the left is the Joiners Hall, built in 1617, now owned by the National Trust. The rich ornamental wood carving was done by local craftsman Humphrey Beckham, whose memorial is in the Church of St. Thomas'. The street has many fine Georgian-fronted houses down the left-hand side.

54. At the top of St. Anne's Street across the dual carriageway of the link road is St. Martin's Church, older than the cathedral! Built largely of flint it stands on the site of an even older church. Opposite is the little school for the very small children.

Published by W. Jukes, Wilton

WESLEYAN CHAPEL, CHURCH STREET.

55. Salisbury has always been an important centre of religion, and all denominations are well represented in the city with their various churches and chapels. The Wesleyan Chapel in Church Street is a rather impressive building with noble windows and curved portico, and a finely decorated interior.

56. The Salvation Army has a special claim to fame in Salisbury for their very first band was created here in the city by Charles Fry and a few others in 1878. Soon the band had expanded to muster over 36 musicians as we see here on this postcard of around 1900. Maybe a relative will recognise an early member of their family proudly clutching their gleaming instruments.

57. Retracing our steps to the centre of the town at the southern end of Queen Street there is a cross-roads. To the east is Milford Street with some very nice old hotels and coaching inns and on the corner there used to be in 1890 Wilkes the ironmongers, alas burned down in 1937, now a modern store is on this site.

58. Turning west at that same cross-roads you enter the New Canal. Here was the wool market on the north side of this wide street, where now motor coaches plying the old carrier routes bring in country folk from the surrounding villages. Opposite on the other side is a lovely old timber-fronted building known as the Hall of John Halle. In this postcard the long dresses suggest the year to be about 1910.

Salisbury, Ye Halle of John Halle

59. Here it is, the Hall of John Halle, who was a wealthy woolmerchant and built the hall as a home and place of work in 1495. He was mayor of Salisbury several times, always at odds with the Bishop, but eventually he settled down. Later his home became a china warehouse, and the firm occupying the shop in this old postcard is still in business in the city. Today however this hall is now our cinema!

60. This picture, taken in 1949, shows the Hall as the entrance to the Gaumont Palace cinema. In 1929 an announcement was made that a cinema was to be built at the rear of the ancient hall. In 1931 it opened, and the wise architects appreciated that the transition from mediaeval entrance hall to a modern cinema would be too much of a cultural shock so the auditorium was created in the Tudor style to harmonise with the ancient vestibule.

ENTRANCE HALL OF THE GAUMONT PICTURE PALACE, FORMERLY
THE BANQUETING-HALL OF JOHN HALLE
Built 1470.   Restored by Pugin, 1834

61. The inside of the hall as the foyer to the cinema is seen in this artist drawing by R. Grundy Heape, done in the early 1930's. It shows the fine hammer-beam roof and carved wooden screen surrounding the three entrance doors leading to the inner foyer of the new cinema. On either side there are splendid stain glass windows.

62. From this picture of the interior of the cinema in 1931 you can see how the architects went to much trouble to make the decor of the auditorium in keeping with the entrance, with painted tapestries on the walls, and a superb stage curtain showing scenes from mediaeval history. After the premier of Lawrence Olivier's film of 'Henry V' in 1944 at the Carlton cinema in London the stage curtains especially made for that premier depicting the Battle of Agincourt were sent down to Salisbury as the natural permanent home for such historic curtains.

63. During the opening week of the Gaumont Palace in September 1931 the proud manager and his forty members of staff, who were to serve the public within this lovely cinema, paraded outside the entrance for a group photograph. Today this cinema still serves the public as a triple cinema complex, and upstairs in the balcony the original auditorium is much the same as on opening day.

Salisbury, St. Thomas' Church.

64. Walking westwards from the cinema we turn right back into the High Street, and at the northern end we see St. Thomas' Church, the parish church, built about 1200 so that those building the cathedral could use it as place of worship. A peel of bells is still rung from this recently restored bell tower.

Salisbury, St Thomas' Church

65. Inside St. Thomas' Church the light and airy
interior shows up much interesting woodwork in the
roof, stone carving and wall paintings, and best of all
above the chancel arch a superb 'Doom' painting,
depicting Christ on high with souls of the departed
either reaching up towards him or sadly falling to less
pleasant regions! There is much to see and linger over
in this lovely church.

St. Thomas Churchyard, Salisbury

66. Outside St. Thomas' is the old churchyard in the quiet secluded corner tucked away behind the busy streets, only a few yards from the turmoil of traffic. Here are the backs of the Haunch of Venison in Queen Street, Stevens tobacco factory in Silver Street. Royalists and Roundheads skirmished in these alleys during the Civil War of 1649.

52 SALISBURY. - The Clock Tower and Infirmary.

67. Leaving St. Thomas' turn right along Bridge Street and you come to Fisherton Bridge and the clock tower, built on the site of the old city gaol. Beyond on the left is the hospital built by John Wood, builder of Georgian Bath. The river beneath is the Avon and looking over the right parapet you will see the thirteenth century Bishop's Mill. This picture was taken about 1910.

Church House & Crane Bridge, Salisbury.

M. J. R. — B. No 2207

68. Looking again over the left hand parapet of Fisherton Bridge you will see downstream another bridge, Crane Bridge, widened considerably since this postcard was taken. From here footpaths lead along the river bank into Elizabeth Gardens laid out in 1953 to commemorate the coronation of Elizabeth II. The big house is Church House, the headquarters of the cathedral administration.

69. Walking ahead from Fisherton Bridge we enter Fisherton Street, always a busy thoroughfare leading to the railway station. The Angel Temperance Hotel on the right has gone, the store on the left is now very much smaller, and ahead on the right can just be seen the original Picture House.

70. In the early part of the century Fisherton Street was always liable to serious flooding. Out would come the horse and carts to ferry people through the water, as well as helping hands from the policeman who, unlike the man on the right, is as you would expect well prepared with high boots. Today due to efficient river control flooding rarely occurs on this scale.

71. Looking back the other way down Fisherton Street we can see one of the early cinemas, the Picture House, which opened in 1916. This picture, taken on 18th June 1928, lures audiences in with a silent movie of 'The Loves of Carmen' with 1920's heart-throb Victor McLaglen and Dolores del Rio. The frontage had a pleasing iron work canopy and gas lamps. The building was demolished in 1978.

72. The same cinema even earlier on Peace Day 21st July 1919. The staff are gathered outside to celebrate the great day. The usherettes in their caps and aprons suggest the tea tray may be passed along to your seat during the performance, but in fact here is no record of such delightful favours being presented to their patrons.

73. When the old original Picture House closed a brand new Picture House opened next door in 1937, and gave excellent service to the public for nearly 25 years before being sold to the City Council and converted into the City Hall, in memory of those servicemen from Salisbury who gave their lives in the Second World War.

74. Almost opposite the City Hall there used to be a splendid fish and game shop with an art nouveau frontage as this drawing from the Salisbury College of Art shows. For several years the façade had been hidden behind a modern frontage, in fact it was thought to have been demolished, but quite recently a new owner uncovered the original shop front and hopes to restore it.

75. At the end of Fisherton Street you come to the railway station. Salisbury has always been an important railway centre, in the days of steam as many as fifty engines would be ready with steam up to take the long distance expresses on westwards to sunny Devon, or eastwards to smoky London. Today the footbridge across the platforms and the engine sheds have all gone but it still remains an important junction linking the south coast to Wales and the Midlands.

THE RAILWAY DISASTER AT SALISBURY, JULY, 1ST., 1906.
F. FUTCHER, PHOTO. 19, FISHERTON ST.

76. Disaster happened on 1st July 1906. A boat train from Plymouth to London took the bend at high speed and went over the bridge into Fisherton Street below killing 28 passengers. Ever since then a company rule was brought in making all trains in both directions stop at Salisbury station.

77. No doubt because of such disasters as we saw in the last picture the Salisbury branch of the railway-man's union devoted great efforts for the protection of the widows and orphans of those left behind after railway staff had been killed in such disasters. This postcard of the Salisbury branch dates about 1920.

78. Every town has its share of disasters and Salisbury was no exception, especially from fire with all the old timber houses. Even the old Salisbury steam laundry which you might have thought would have been difficult to catch fire, burned down in the 1920's much to the excitement next morning of the children.

Victoria Park, Salisbury

3288

Valentines Series

79. All was not always disaster, or perhaps to escape from them, the townspeople needed to relax and so Victoria Park was created to the north of the city on the road to Amesbury and Old Sarum. Constructed in 1887 to commemorate Queen Victoria's silver jubilee this card shows the early stages of planting, and young growth of the now huge trees in this park.

Salisbury Victoria Park.

80. The same park a few years later with the trees now much sturdier and the ladies out with their children and prams obviously enjoying a spell of hot sunshine. Today tennis courts, bowling and putting greens, and football, as well as pleasant shady walks, all offer their pleasures amidst the colourful flower-filled beds, making the park a haven of pleasure for young and old.

the Cathedral from the Greencroft, Salisbury.

81. Another popular open space is aptly named the Greencroft and lies close to the eastern side of the town. Children have played here down the years although it did have a commercial use in the middle-ages when cloth was made in the city, and laid out to dry on the Greencroft, 'Wiltshire Whites' the cloth was called and was much in demand in London.

82. If you wandered a mile or two out on to the hills around Salisbury in the late 1800's you soon came to cornfields, and here high on Laverstock down the harvesting of the golden grain is taking place with the spire of the cathedral seen through the heat haze down in the valley below. Does anyone recognise perhaps their great-grandfather here in this picture?

River Avon, Salisbury

83. Throughout the city there are numerous delightful riverside walks along the banks of the five rivers and their many tributaries that criss-cross the town. In this picture the Avon flows past the rear gardens of the houses at the back of Castle Street, where once the wool and felt used to be processed. No doubt still today these river banks are popular with those desirous of a little privacy!

The Riverside Walk, Salisbury.

84. Out on the south eastern side of the city the very pleasant Riverside Walk, now known as Churchill Gardens, was developed at the turn of the century as a leisure area, and made a safe and pleasant spot for young children to play alongside the Avon flowing downstream towards Downton and Fordingbridge, and eventually the sea at Christchurch. Notice the policeman keeping a wary eye on the safety of the children.

85. Perhaps the most popular and famous riverside walk is via Crane Street, through Elizabeth Gardens, to Constable's Bridge across the Nadder, leading to the town path to Harnham. On this bridge John Constable is said to have set up his easel and created his masterpiece of the cathedral framed within a rainbow. A favourite haunt for generations of young anglers catching 'tiddlers' in jam jars.

86. Today the bridge is arched and rarely floods, unlike this picture of serious flooding in the 1920's. It would have taken a brave person to have endeavoured to have reached Harnham by this route in these conditions. Fortunately today expert flood control seems capable of dealing with heavy storms and rapidly rising waters — or so we hope!

87. Here again the waters have risen fast and flow in waves down Water Lane connecting Fisherton Street with Mill Road. No wonder in the middle-ages Salisbury was called the 'Venice of southern England'. A little too like Venice for comfort in this picture of the floods in January 1915.

THE CATHEDRAL AND OLD MILL. SALISBURY.   30009

88. Here at Harnham Mill at the end of the town path water is not quite such of a problem, and children love to come to this spot to feed the ducks whilst parents perhaps find hospitality dispensed at the old mill itself. The views across the water meadows to the cathedral somehow epitomise the spirit of Salisbury, the graceful spire a tribute to God as it soars high above his bounty in the fields below.

89. The more energetic amongst you may well wish to carry on from Harnham Mill and climb to the top of Harnham hill and walk along the path at the top which gives magnificient views of the city below across to the far hills to the north and Old Sarum. The stairway cut into the chalk hillside is still there and brings you down into the village of Harnham itself.

HARNHAM BRIDGE, SALISBURY.

90. Here in this village on the banks of the Avon is a famous hostelry, and a fitting place to pause for rest and refreshment, in whose riverside gardens you can linger and enjoy the view. Often on a summers evening a group of local songsters will anchor in midstream and charmingly cast their voices across the stream and entertain you with their music. Our family group in the picture seem to taking a welcome cup of tea.

HARNHAM BRIDGE & SALISBURY CATHEDRAL

91. We return to the city by crossing the ancient road bridge built by Bishop Bingham in 1244, and by that act made Salisbury prosperous and Wilton the poorer. Here writer Anthony Trollope pondered as he leaned upon the parapet and gazed around, and so was born Barchester and the lives and loves of the gaitered clergy that dwelt within the Cathedral Close.

Harnham Bridge, Salisbury

92. Upon the bridge itself we see a sight that must have indeed been common since the bridge was built, the flocks of sheep coming from market and being herded towards the rich green pastures atop the chalk hills all around. Again a handy policeman seems to be helping the shepherd so that the motor bike and side-car can get past. Today a new wide road bridge downstream diverts the traffic from this peaceful backwater.

ST. NICHOLAS HOSPITAL & CHAPEL, SALISBURY.

Homer, Post Office, Harnham Rd.   Photo by Jukes. Wilton.

93. To the left of the bridge lies St. Nicholas' Hospital, the inspiration for Hiram's Hospital in Anthony Trollope's first book in the Barchester series of novels: 'The Warden'. Today enlarged and modernised it still gives sanctuary to the aged members of the church and community.

94. Salisbury has quite a rich musical and literary history and over on the western outskirts of the city on the lower road to Wilton lies the hamlet of Bemerton, where poet and parson George Herbert had his church and rectory. Along the paths and across the little bridges through the lovely water meadows leading to the cathedral he would wander slowly, marvelling at the beauty around him, giving him inspiration for his hymns and poems.

Wilton Road, Salisbury.

95. The main road from Salisbury to Wilton in the early 1900's was a tree-lined avenue that lead invitingly to the ancient town of Wilton, once the capital of Wiltonshire, shortened to the modern word of Wiltshire. It was the third oldest borough in England, and only lost its importance when trade moved to Salisbury when the bridge was built lower downstream across the Avon, making Wilton into a backwater.

WILTON HOUSE, SALISBURY.

96. Wilton House, home of the Earl of Pembroke, is a fine example of the work of Renaissance architect Inigo Jones, built originally on the site of a Benedictine Abbey. Within is the famous 'double-cube' room and a host of fine paintings by Rembrandt and Vandyke. The public can visit the house and lovely grounds with its Palladian bridge across the Nadder, most of the year.

The Wilton Royal Carpet Factory.

FINE REAL AXMINSTER CARPET. 60ft. x 50ft.

97. The Wilton Royal Carpet Factory, famous the world over, is still making carpets after 400 years of production, and the factory itself is a group of eighteenth century and modern buildings surrounding a pleasant courtyard, here used to advantage to display and work on a giant carpet, obviously destined for a stately home, the year about 1900. Today tours can be taken round the factory to see the work in progress.

98. Another stately home near to Salisbury is Longford Castle. It is situated about two miles out of the city southwards on the Bournemouth road. Occasionally it is open to the public by special arrangement, again it houses beautiful paintings and furniture, and in its extensive grounds there is now a thriving fish farm famous for the quality of its trout.

99. Pepper Box hill is a lovely open area of downland high up on the hills along the Southampton road eight miles from Salisbury. From its vantage point you can see the sea between Southampton and the Isle of Wight. The brick tower is a folly built in 1600 by a local farmer who was jealous of all the great mansions around and decided to build his own lookout tower (and why not?). Today it has become his own monument.

Eyres Folly (or the "Pepper Box"). built A.D. 1600, near Whiteparish

3623. SALISBURY OPEN SWIMMING BATH. COPYRIGHT.

100. Salisbury swimmers, being nearly thirty miles from the sea, had to make do with pools fed by the fresh running streams all around. Here in 1920 the old swimming pool used to be just behind the Bishop's Mill in St. Thomas' Square. Today there is a fine warmed indoor pool that gives a few degrees of extra comfort to less hardy swimmers than we see in this old picture.

101. To go to the seaside in the 1920's was a favourite outing for most people in Salisbury, usually it meant hiring a char-a-banc just like this one. Many a happy party started their day just outside the china shop in the New Canal that became the Gaumont Palace cinema. I hope those large hats were securely fastened to their charming wearers! Notice the speed limit of 12 miles per hour on the side of the vehicle.

102. Here is another delightful sixteen seater char-a-banc about to set out on a jaunt to the sea from the Roebuck Inn in the New Canal where the wool market used to be. It says 'Queen of the West' on the front. I still worry about all those hats when bowling along the roads open to the wind. If it rains there is a hood at the back but no windows! But what fun it must have been! Thanks to Alan Alexander for the use of this postcard.

103. Although the advertisement on the side of this 1920's bus recommends a trip to Mars the bus itself was scheduled for a destination much nearer, Wilton in fact, and the various residential districts on the city's outskirts that were developing rapidly. It must have been tough going on top on a winter's night, but quite delightful on hot summer days. The same company still operates the local services today.

SALISBURY

Stonehenge.

104. Stonehenge lies close to Salisbury and makes a fascinating place to visit for countless thousands of local as well as overseas visitors. At the time of this picture you could wander among the stones and picnic, sheep would graze alongside them, and here urgent repair work seems to be underway, again a lone policeman guards the ancient monument built 5,000 years ago, and still today on midsummer morning thousands gather at dawn to celebrate with the Druids the rising of the sun, in truth, the dawn of eternity.

SALISBURY

R.H.A. Camp, Beacon Hill, Bulford.

105. On the chalk uplands all around Stonehenge the army has been using the wide open spaces as a training ground ever since the days of the Crimean War in Victorian times. Great camps of canvas were erected for the troops of the First World War, replaced with permanent army barracks in later years.

GRAND REVIEW AT PERHAM DOWN, SALISBURY PLAIN.
PHOTO BY: T.L. FULLER. AMESBURY.

106. Not only the army, but the air force too have used the Plain for training, and pioneers of civil aviation found the clear terrain ideal for training pilots. Sir Alan Cobham, the greatest pioneer of flying, used to bring his famous air circus to Salisbury. Every year air displays and reviews, such as this picture shows, would be held to promote interest in this new form of transportation!

2   *SALISBURY. — General View from Spire of Cathedral.*

107. But we do not have to fly in order to see Salisbury from on high, you just have to climb the cathedral spire and see the superb view from there. Our picture of 1910 shows a much smaller Salisbury than we would see today, very few of the residential areas had yet been planned. Let us finish this journey round Salisbury by going back down from the spire into the cathedral choir.

Salisbury.
Choral Evensong

108. Thank you for joining me on this journey round
my home town. What better way to finish than to
sing with the choir at Evensong. You quickly realise
this great cathedral is no cold lifeless thing, but a
living creation of stone dedicated to the service of
God. Within this monument to Christ music and
prayer combine to say that 'Good-the more communi-
cated the more abundant grows'. So with imagina-
tion, vitality, and love it endeavours to spread its
Christian message to all those who may care to
recognise it. Good bye, come and visit us again.